Winter Soup: Hot and Hear You Lose Weight V

by **Alissa N**
Text copyright(c)2015 Alissa Noel Grey

All rights reserved. No part of this publication may be reproduced, distributed, or transmitted in any form or by any means, including photocopying, recording, or other electronic or mechanical methods, without the prior written permission of the publisher, except in the case of brief quotations embodied in critical reviews and certain other noncommercial uses permitted by copyright law

Although every precaution has been taken to verify the accuracy of the information contained herein, the author and publisher assume no responsibility for any errors or omissions. No liability is assumed for damages that may result from the use of information contained within.

Table Of Contents

Warm Up With a Bowl of Something Delicious	5
Healthy Italian Chicken Soup	6
Chicken and Butternut Squash Soup	7
Old-Fashioned Chicken Soup	8
Creamy Chicken Soup	9
Broccoli and Chicken Soup	10
French Onion Soup	11
Goulash Soup	13
Italian Beef and Vegetable Soup	14
Barley Beef Soup	15
German Barley Soup	16
Split Pea Soup with Ham and Barley	17
Hearty Meatball Soup	18
Lentil and Beef Soup	20
Turkey and Ricotta Meatball Soup	22
Mushroom and Kale Soup	23
Brussels Sprout and Tomato Soup	24
Indian Chickpea Soup	25
Creamy Broccoli and Potato Soup	26
Creamy Brussels Sprout Soup	27
Creamy Potato Soup	28
Leek, Brown Rice and Potato Soup	29
Mediterranean Chickpea Soup	30
Carrot, Sweet Potato and Chickpea Soup	31
Sweet Potato and Coconut Soup	32
Creamy Tomato and Roasted Pepper Soup	33
Italian Egg Drop Soup	34
Fresh Asparagus Soup	35
Creamy Artichoke Soup	36
Creamy Parsnip Soup	37
Fast Red Lentil Soup	38
Mediterranean Lentil Soup	39
Carrot and Chickpea Soup	41
Celery, Apple and Carrot Soup	42
Pea, Dill and Rice Soup	43

Minted Pea and Nettle Soup	44
Bean and Pasta Soup	45
Tuscan Bean Soup	46
Lima Bean Soup	47
Mediterranean Lentil and Chickpea Soup	48
Curried Lentil and Parsnip Soup	49
Italian Vegetable Soup	50
French Vegetable Soup	51
Spiced Beet and Carrot Soup	52
Creamy Cauliflower Soup	53
Pumpkin and Bell Pepper Soup	54
Mushroom Soup	55
Spinach Soup	56
Brown Lentil Soup	57
Quinoa, Sweet Potato and Tomato Soup	58
Leek and Quinoa Soup	60
Red Lentil and Quinoa Soup	61
Spinach and Quinoa Soup	62
Vegetable Quinoa Soup	63
Tomato and Quinoa Soup	64
Kale, Leek and Quinoa Soup	65
Carrot, Sweet Potato and Chickpea Soup	66
FREE BONUS RECIPES: 20 Superfood Paleo and Vegan Smoothies for Vibrant Health and Easy Weight Loss	67
Kale and Kiwi Smoothie	68
Delicious Broccoli Smoothie	69
Papaya Smoothie	70
Beet and Papaya Smoothie	71
Lean Green Smoothie	72
Easy Antioxidant Smoothie	73
Healthy Purple Smoothie	74
Mom's Favorite Kale Smoothie	75
Creamy Green Smoothie	76
Strawberry and Arugula Smoothie	77
Emma's Amazing Smoothie	78
Good-To-Go Morning Smoothie	79

Endless Energy Smoothie	80
High-fiber Fruit Smoothie	81
Nutritious Green Smoothie	82
Apricot, Strawberry and Banana Smoothie	83
Spinach and Green Apple Smoothie	84
Superfood Blueberry Smoothie	85
Zucchini and Blueberry Smoothie	86
Tropical Spinach Smoothie	87

Warm Up With a Bowl of Something Delicious

When it comes to soup, its essence is not merely nutritional, but also emotional. A bowl of steaming hot soup has the ability to get us through the not-so-good times; it brings much needed warmth to the long dark winter nights. In fact, soup is the ultimate comfort food during the cold autumn and winter months. I love it and could happily eat it every day. Some of the winter soup recipes in this cookbook are my own while others have been handed down from generation to generation in my extended family and I have personally cooked and tasted them all.

Warm up and fill up with my easy, feel-good winter soups that are healthier versions of traditional soup recipes. They are high in fiber, low in fat and are prepared with superfood veggies and legumes, lean chicken and beef, and healthy nuts and spices.

Oh, and they taste delicious, too!

Healthy Italian Chicken Soup

Serves: 4

Prep time: 35 min

Ingredients:

3 chicken breasts

1 carrot, chopped

1 small zucchini, peeled and chopped

1 celery stalk, chopped

1 small onion, chopped

1 bay leaf

5 cups water

6-7 black olives, pitted and halved

1/2 tsp salt

1 tsp dried basil

black pepper, to taste

fresh parsley, to serve

lemon juice, to serve

Directions:

Place chicken breasts, onion, carrot, celery and bay leaf in a deep soup pot. Add in salt, black pepper, basil and water. Stir well and bring to a boil. Add zucchini and olives and reduce heat. Simmer for 30 minutes.

Remove chicken from the pot and set aside to cool. Shred it and return it back to the pot. Serve with lemon juice and sprinkled with parsley.

Chicken and Butternut Squash Soup

Serves: 4

Prep time: 35 min

Ingredients:

3 boneless chicken thighs, diced

1/2 onion, chopped

6-7 white mushrooms, chopped

1 small zucchini, peeled and diced

1 cup butternut squash, diced

1 tbsp tomato paste

5 cups water

1/4 tsp cumin

1 tbsp paprika

3 tbsp extra virgin olive oil

Directions:

In a deep soup pot, heat olive oil and gently sauté onion, stirring occasionally. Add chicken and cook for 2-3 minutes. Stir in cumin, paprika and butternut squash.

Dilute the tomato paste in a cup of water and add to the soup. Add in the remaining water and bring to a boil.

Reduce heat and simmer for 10 minutes then add zucchini and mushrooms. Simmer until butternut squash is tender. Season with salt and black pepper to taste.

Old-Fashioned Chicken Soup

Serves: 4

Prep time: 35 min

Ingredients:

3 boneless chicken tights, chopped

1 small onion, chopped

3 garlic cloves

1 potato, skinned and diced

1 large carrot, chopped

1 red bell pepper, chopped

1 celery stalk, chopped

1/2 cup vermicelli

1 bay leaf

1 tsp salt

1/2 cup fresh parsley leaves, finely cut

black pepper, to taste

Directions:

Place the chicken, bay leaf, celery, carrot, onion, red pepper, sweet potato and salt into a pot with 5 cups of cold water.

Bring to the boil, reduce heat and simmer for 30 minutes. Stir in vermicelli, season with salt and pepper, add in parsley, and simmer for 2-3 minutes.

Serve with lemon juice or Greek yogurt.

Creamy Chicken Soup

Serves: 4

Prep time: 35 min

Ingredients:

4 chicken breasts

1 carrot, chopped

1 cup zucchini, peeled and chopped

2 cups cauliflower, broken into florets

1 celery rib, chopped

1 small onion, chopped

5 cups water

1/2 tsp salt

black pepper, to taste

Directions:

Place chicken breasts, onion, carrot, celery, cauliflower and zucchini in a deep soup pot. Add in salt, black pepper and 5 cups of water. Stir and bring to a boil.

Simmer for 30 minutes then remove chicken from the pot and let it cool slightly.

Blend soup until completely smooth. Shred or dice the chicken meat, return it back to the pot, stir and serve.

Broccoli and Chicken Soup

Serves: 4

Prep time: 35 min

Ingredients:

4 boneless chicken thighs, diced

1 small carrot, chopped

1 broccoli head, broken into florets

1 garlic clove, chopped

1 small onion, chopped

4 cups water

3 tbsp extra virgin olive oil

1/2 tsp salt

black pepper, to taste

Directions:

In a deep soup pot, heat olive oil and gently sauté broccoli for 2-3 minutes, stirring occasionally. Add in onion, carrot, chicken and cook, stirring, for 2-3 minutes. Stir in salt, black pepper and water.

Bring to a boil. Simmer for 30 minutes then remove from heat and set aside to cool.

In a blender or food processor, blend soup until completely smooth. Serve and enjoy!

French Onion Soup

Serves: 5-6

Prep time: 80 min

Ingredients:

6 large onions, peeled and thinly sliced

1 small onion, chopped

2 garlic cloves, minced

5 cups beef broth

1/2 cup dry white wine

1 tsp sugar

3 tbsp extra virgin olive oil

2 bay leaves

1 tsp dried thyme

1 cup grated Swiss Gruyère

black pepper and salt, to taste

8 slices of French baguette

Directions:

In a skillet, heat olive oil on medium heat. Add the onions and toss to coat with the olive oil. Cook, stirring often, until they have softened, about 20 minutes. Increase the heat to medium high and cook, stirring often, until the onions start to brown, about 10 more minutes. Sprinkle with sugar and salt and continue to cook until the onions are well browned, about 15 more minutes. Stir in the minced garlic and cook until just fragrant - 1 minute more.

Add the wine to the skillet and scrape up the browned bits on the bottom and sides, deglazing it as you go.

Transfer everything to a soup pot and add the beef broth, bay leaves, and thyme. Bring to a gentle boil, cover, and lower the heat. Simmer for about 30 minutes. Discard the bay leaves.

While the soup is simmering, line a baking sheet with foil and preheat the oven to 450 F with a rack in the upper third of the oven.

Brush both sides of the baguette slices lightly with olive oil. Toast until lightly browned, about 4-5 minutes. Sprinkle with the grated Gruyère cheese, return to the oven and bake until the cheese is bubbly.

Ladle soup into bowl and top with one cheesy toast onto the top of each bowl of soup.

Goulash Soup

Serves: 4-5

Prep time: 100 min

Ingredients:

12 oz beef stew meat, cut into 1 inch cubes

1 carrot, chopped

2 cloves garlic, finely chopped

1 small onion, chopped

4-5 potatoes, peeled and cubed

1 can tomatoes, diced and undrained

2 tbsp olive oil

4-5 tbsp sour cream, to serve

Directions:

In a large soup pot, heat olive oil and cook beef until browned. Add onion, garlic and carrot. Cook for 3-4 minutes until fragrant. Stir in the tomatoes and beef broth.

Bring to a boil then reduce heat and simmer for about one hour until the beef is tender. Add the potatoes. Cook, partially covered, for about 30 minutes more until slightly thickened.

Serve with a dollop of sour cream.

Italian Beef and Vegetable Soup

Serves: 4-5

Prep time: 40 min

Ingredients:

2 slices bacon, chopped

1 lb lean ground beef

1 carrot, chopped

2 cloves garlic, finely chopped

1 small onion, chopped

1 celery stalk, chopped

1 bay leaf

1 tsp dried basil

1 cup canned tomatoes, diced and drained

4 cups beef broth

1/2 cup canned chickpeas

½ cup vermicelli

Directions:

In a large soup pot, cook bacon and ground beef until well done, breaking up the beef as it cooks. Drain off the fat and add in onion, garlic, carrot and celery. Cook for 3-4 minutes until fragrant.

Stir in the bay leaf, basil, tomatoes and beef broth. Bring to a boil then reduce heat and simmer for about 20 minutes. Add the chickpeas and vermicelli.

Cook uncovered, for about 5 minutes more and serve.

Barley Beef Soup

Serves: 4-5

Prep time: 80 min

Ingredients:

12 oz beef stew meat, cut into 1 inch cubes

1 medium leek, chopped

2 garlic cloves, chopped

2 bay leaves

1 can tomatoes (15 oz), diced and drained

1/2 cup barley

1 cup frozen mixed vegetables

4 cups beef broth

3 tbsp extra virgin olive oil

1 tsp paprika

Directions:

Heat oil in a large saucepan over medium-high heat. Sauté beef cubes until well browned. Add in leeks and garlic and sauté until fragrant. Add paprika, beef broth and bay leaves; season with salt and pepper.

Cover and bring to a boil then reduce heat and simmer for 60 minutes.

Stir in the frozen vegetables, tomatoes, and barley. Return to boiling, reduce heat and simmer, covered, about 15 minutes more or until meat and vegetables are tender. Discard bay leaves and serve.

German Barley Soup

Serves: 4-5

Prep time: 40 min

Ingredients:

1 German sausage, like bockwurst or bratwurst, thinly sliced

1 bacon, chopped

1 cup barley

1/2 onion, chopped

1 carrot, finely chopped

1 leek, finely chopped

1 celery stalk, finely chopped

4 cups beef broth

3 tbsp butter

1 tsp paprika

1 tsp nutmeg

Directions:

Heat butter in a large saucepan over medium-high heat. Sauté onion until transparent. Add in barley and cook, stirring, until lightly toasted. Add paprika, nutmeg, beef broth, leek, carrot, celery, sausages and bacon; season with salt and pepper.

Bring to a boil then reduce heat and simmer for 35 minutes, stirring occasionally, until sausage is tender.

Split Pea Soup with Ham and Barley

Serves: 4-5

Prep time: 35 min

Ingredients:

3/4 cup dry yellow split peas

2 carrots, chopped

1/2 lb low-sodium, nitrate-free, lean cooked ham, cut into 1/2-inch cubes

1 zucchini, peeled and diced

1 potato, peeled and diced

1 cup quick-cooking pearl barley

2 tsp dried sage

4 cups water

4 tbsp extra virgin olive oil

salt and black pepper, to taste

Directions:

In a medium pot, bring 2 cups water to a boil on high heat. Add split peas and reduce heat to medium-low. Simmer, uncovered, for 20 minutes. Drain and set aside.

Gently heat olive oil in a large soup pot. Add in onions, carrot and ham and cook for 1-2 minutes, stirring, until vegetables are tender.

Add in zucchini, sage, barley and water. Season to taste with salt and pepper and simmer for 15 minutes.

Hearty Meatball Soup

Serves: 4-5

Prep time: 35 min

Ingredients:

1 lb lean ground beef

1 egg, lightly whisked

1/2 onion, chopped

2 garlic cloves, chopped

1 tomato, diced

2 potatoes, diced

1/2 red bell pepper, chopped

4 cups water

4 tbsp flour

1 cup vermicelli, broken into pieces

½ bunch of parsley, finely cut

3 tbsp extra virgin olive oil

½ tsp black pepper

1 tsp paprika

1 tsp salt

Directions:

Place ground meat, egg, black pepper and salt in a bowl. Combine well with hands and roll teaspoonfuls of the mixture into balls. Place flour in a shallow bowl and roll each meatball in the flour then set aside on a large plate.

Heat olive oil into a deep soup pot and gently sauté onion and garlic until transparent. Add water and bring to a boil. Stir in meatballs, carrot, pepper, tomato and potatoes. Reduce heat to low and simmer, uncovered, for 15 minutes.

Add parsley and vermicelli and cook for 5 more minutes. Serve with a dollop of yogurt on top.

Lentil and Beef Soup

Serves 6

Prep time: 40 min

Ingredients:

1 lb ground beef

1 cup dry green lentils

1 large carrot, chopped

1 onion, chopped

2 garlic cloves, chopped

1 potato, peeled and diced

2 garlic cloves, chopped

1 tomato, grated

4 cups vegetable broth

1/2 tsp oregano

1 tsp smoked paprika

2 tbsp extra virgin olive oil

salt and black pepper, to taste

1/2 cup fresh parsley leaves, finely cut, to serve

Directions:

In a soup pot, heat the olive oil and gently brown the ground beef, breaking it up with a spoon.

Stir in garlic paprika, oregano and lentils. Add remaining vegetables and vegetable broth. Bring to a boil.

Reduce heat to low and simmer, covered, for about 30 minutes, or until the lentils are tender. Sprinkle with parsley and serve.

Turkey and Ricotta Meatball Soup

Serves: 4-5

Prep time: 35 min

Ingredients:

1 lb ground turkey meat

1 egg, lightly whisked

1 cup whole milk ricotta

1 cup grated Parmesan cheese

4 tbsp flour

1/2 onion, finely cut

4 cups chicken broth

2 cups baby spinach leaves

1 tsp dried thyme leaves

3 tbsp extra virgin olive oil

½ tsp black pepper

Directions:

Place ground turkey meat, Ricotta, Parmesan, egg and black pepper. Combine well with hands and roll teaspoonfuls of the mixture into balls. Place flour in a shallow bowl and roll each meatball in the flour then set aside on a large plate.

Heat olive oil into a deep soup pot and gently sauté onion until transparent. Add in thyme and broth and bring to a boil. Stir in meatballs, reduce heat, and simmer, uncovered, for 15 minutes. Add baby spinach and cook for 2-3 more minutes until it wilts.

Mushroom and Kale Soup

Serves: 4-5

Prep time: 30 min

Ingredients:

1 onion, chopped

1 carrot, chopped

1 zucchini, peeled and diced

1 potato, peeled and diced

10 white mushrooms, chopped

1 bunch kale (10 oz), stemmed and coarsely chopped

3 cups vegetable broth

4 tbsp extra virgin olive oil

salt and black pepper. to taste

Directions:

Gently heat olive oil in a large soup pot. Add in onions, carrot and mushrooms and cook until vegetables are tender.

Stir in the zucchini, kale and vegetable broth. Season to taste with salt and pepper and simmer for 20 minutes.

Brussels Sprout and Tomato Soup

Serves 4

Prep time: 20 min

Ingredients:

3 cups Brussels sprouts, halved

3 large tomatoes, diced

1 onion, chopped

2-3 garlic cloves, chopped

1 tsp sugar

3 cups vegetable broth

3 tbsp extra virgin olive oil

1 tsp paprika

salt and black pepper, to taste

Directions:

Gently heat the olive oil in a deep soup pot and sauté onion, garlic and paprika, stirring, for 2-3 minutes or until tender.

Add in the diced tomatoes and vegetable broth. Cover and bring to the boil, then reduce heat to low and simmer, stirring occasionally, for 5 minutes.

Remove from heat and blend until smooth. Return to the soup pot, add in Brussels sprouts and simmer for 15 minutes more.

Season with salt and pepper to taste before serving.

Indian Chickpea Soup

Serves: 4-5

Prep time: 20 min

Ingredients:

2 carrots, chopped

1 small onion, chopped

1 cup green beans, chopped

1 garlic clove, minced

1 can chickpeas, undrained

4 cups vegetable broth

3-4 tbsp extra virgin olive oil

1 tbsp garam masala

1 tsp finely grated fresh root ginger

salt and black pepper, to taste

naan bread, to serve

Directions:

Heat olive oil in a deep soup pot over medium-high heat. Gently sauté onion, garlic and carrots for 3-4 minutes, stirring. Add in ginger and gram masala and cook for 1 minute more, stirring.

Add vegetable broth and chickpeas. Bring to the boil then reduce heat and simmer, covered, for 15 minutes.

Blend soup until smooth and return to pan. Add in green beans and cook over medium-high heat for 3-5 minutes.

Season with salt and pepper to taste, and serve with naan bread.

Creamy Broccoli and Potato Soup

Serves: 4-5

Prep time: 30 min

Ingredients:

3 cups broccoli, cut into florets and chopped

2 potatoes, peeled and chopped

1 large onion, chopped

3 garlic cloves, minced

1 cup raw cashews

1 cup vegetable broth

4 cups water

3 tbsp extra virgin olive oil

1/2 tsp ground nutmeg

Directions:

Soak cashews in a bowl covered with water for at least 4 hours. Drain water and blend cashews with 1 cup of vegetable broth until smooth. Set aside.

Gently heat olive oil in a large saucepan over medium-high heat. Cook onion and garlic and for 3-4 minutes until tender. Add in broccoli, potato, nutmeg and water. Cover and bring to the boil, then reduce heat and simmer for 20 minutes, stirring from time to time. Remove from heat and stir in cashew mixture.

Blend until smooth, return to pan and cook until heated through.

Creamy Brussels Sprout Soup

Serves: 4-5

Prep time: 30 min

Ingredients:

1 lb frozen Brussels sprouts, thawed

2 potatoes, peeled and chopped

1 large onion, chopped

3 garlic cloves, minced

1 cup raw cashews

4 cups vegetable broth

3 tbsp extra virgin olive oil

1/2 tsp curry powder

salt and black pepper, to taste

Directions:

Soak cashews in a bowl covered with water for at least 4 hours. Drain water and blend cashews with 1 cup of vegetable broth until smooth. Set aside.

Gently heat olive oil in a large saucepan over medium-high heat. Cook onion and garlic and for 3-4 minutes until tender. Add in Brussels sprouts, potato, curry and vegetable broth.

Cover and bring to a boil, then reduce heat and simmer for 20 minutes, stirring from time to time. Remove from heat and stir in cashew mixture. Blend until smooth, return to pan and cook until heated through.

Creamy Potato Soup

Serves: 4-5

Prep time: 35 min

Ingredients:

6 medium potatoes, cut into small cubes

1 leek, white part only, chopped

1 carrot, chopped

1 zucchini, peeled and chopped

1 celery stalk, chopped

3 cups water

1 cup coconut milk

3 tbsp extra virgin olive oil

salt and black pepper, to taste

Directions:

Gently heat olive oil in a deep saucepan and sauté the onion for 2-3 minutes. Add in potatoes, carrot, zucchini and celery and cook for 2-3 minutes, stirring.

Add in water and salt and bring to a boil, then lower heat and simmer until the vegetables are tender. Blend until smooth, add coconut milk, blend some more and serve.

Leek, Brown Rice and Potato Soup

Serves: 4-5

Prep time: 35 min

Ingredients:

3 potatoes, peeled and diced

2 leeks, finely chopped

1/4 cup brown rice

5 cups water

3 tbsp extra virgin olive oil

lemon juice, to taste

Directions:

Heat olive oil in a deep soup pot and sauté leeks for 3-4 minutes. Add in potatoes and cook for a minute more.

Stir in water, bring to a boil, and the brown rice. Reduce heat and simmer for 30 minutes. Add lemon juice, to taste, and serve.

Mediterranean Chickpea Soup

Serves 5-6

Ingredients:

1 can (15 oz) chickpeas, drained

1 small onion, chopped

2 garlic cloves, minced

1 can (15 oz) tomatoes, diced

2 cups vegetable broth

1 cup milk

3 tbsp extra virgin olive oil

2 bay leaves

1/2 tsp dried oregano

Directions:

Heat olive oil in a deep soup pot and sauté onion and garlic for 1-2 minutes. Add in broth, chickpeas, tomatoes, bay leaves, and oregano.

Bring the soup to a boil then reduce heat and simmer for 20 minutes. Add in milk and cook for 1-2 minutes more.

Set aside to cool, discard the bay leaves and blend until smooth.

Carrot, Sweet Potato and Chickpea Soup

Serves: 4-5

Prep time: 25 min

Ingredients:

4 large carrots, chopped

1 small onion, chopped

1 can (15 oz) chickpeas, undrained

2 sweet potatoes, peeled and diced

4 cups vegetable broth

2 tbsp extra virgin olive oil

1 tsp cumin

1 tsp ginger

Directions:

Heat olive oil in a large saucepan over medium heat. Add onion and carrots and sauté until tender. Add in broth, chickpeas, sweet potato and seasonings.

Bring to a boil then reduce heat and simmer, covered, for 30 minutes. Blend soup until smooth, add coconut milk and cook for 2-3 minutes until heated through.

Sweet Potato and Coconut Soup

Serves: 4-5

Prep time: 25 min

Ingredients:

1 small onion, chopped

2 lb sweet potatoes, peeled and diced

4 cups vegetable broth

1 can coconut milk

2 tbsp extra virgin olive oil

1 tsp nutmeg

Directions:

Heat olive oil in a large saucepan over medium heat. Add onion and sauté until tender. Add in broth, sweet potato and nutmeg.

Bring to a boil then reduce heat and simmer, covered, for 30 minutes. Blend soup until smooth and cook for 2-3 minutes until heated through.

Creamy Tomato and Roasted Pepper Soup

Serves: 4-5

Prep time: 35 min

Ingredients:

1 (12-ounce) jar roasted red peppers, drained and chopped

1 large onion, chopped

2 garlic cloves, minced

4 medium tomatoes, chopped

4 cups vegetable broth

3 tbsp extra virgin olive oil

2 bay leaves

Directions:

Heat olive oil in a large saucepan over medium-high heat and sauté onion for 3-4 minutes, stirring. Add in garlic and sauté until just fragrant.

Stir in the red peppers, bay leaves and tomatoes and simmer for 10 minutes. Add broth, season with salt and pepper and bring to the boil.

Reduce heat and simmer for 20 minutes. Set aside to cool slightly, remove the bay leaves and blend, in batches, until smooth.

Italian Egg Drop Soup

Serves: 4-5

Prep time: 35 min

Ingredients:

1 leek, white part only, chopped

4 cups chicken broth

1 large egg

3 tbsp extra virgin olive oil

1/3 cup finely grated Parmesan cheese

1 cup spinach leaves, cut in ribbons

salt and black pepper, to taste

Directions:

Gently heat olive oil in a deep saucepan and sauté the leek for 2-3 minutes.

Stir in broth and salt and bring to a boil, then lower heat and simmer.

In a medium bowl, whisk together the egg, Parmesan cheese and black pepper.

Once the soup is simmering, stir in the spinach. Pour the cheese egg mixture into the simmering soup and do not stir for 20-30 seconds. Stir the egg mixture into the soup and cook at a gentle simmer for a minute. Serve hot.

Fresh Asparagus Soup

Serves: 4-5

Prep time: 35 min

Ingredients:

2 lb fresh asparagus, cut into 1 inch pieces

1 large onion, chopped

2 garlic cloves, minced

½ cup raw cashews, soaked in warm water for 1 hour

3 cups chicken broth

3 tbsp extra virgin olive oil

lemon juice, to taste

Directions:

Heat olive oil in a large saucepan over medium-high heat and sauté onion for 3-4 minutes, stirring. Add in garlic and sauté until just fragrant. Stir in asparagus and simmer for 5 minutes.

Add broth, season with salt and pepper and bring to the boil. Reduce heat and simmer for 20 minutes. Set aside to cool slightly, add cashews, and blend, in batches, until smooth. Season with lemon juice and serve.

Creamy Artichoke Soup

Serves: 4-5

Prep time: 35 min

Ingredients:

6 slices bacon

3 cups artichoke hearts, chopped

1/2 onion, chopped

1 celery stalk, chopped

1 small potato, peeled and chopped

2 garlic cloves, minced

2 cups vegetable broth

1 cup milk

2 tbsp extra virgin olive oil

1 tsp salt

black pepper, to serve

Directions:

In a skillet, cook bacon until crisp. Drain on paper towels; set aside. Coarsely chop bacon and place in a microwave-safe pie plate. Drizzle bacon with honey; cover with plastic wrap. Just before serving, cook in the microwave for 30 seconds.

Heat olive oil in a large pot and gently sauté the onion, celery and garlic until just fragrant. Stir in vegetable broth, milk, artichokes and salt and bring to the boil.

Reduce heat and simmer for 30 minutes. Set aside to cool and blend until smooth. Serve sprinkled with black pepper and bacon.

Creamy Parsnip Soup

Serves: 4-5

Prep time: 35 min

Ingredients:

6 slices bacon

5 parsnips, peeled and chopped

1/2 onion, chopped

1 small celery stalk, chopped

1 small potato, peeled and chopped

2 garlic cloves, minced

4 cups vegetable broth

2 tbsp extra virgin olive oil

black pepper, to serve

1 tbsp fresh thyme leaves, to serve

1 cup croûtons, to serve

Directions:

In a skillet, cook bacon until crisp. Drain on paper towels; set aside. Coarsely chop bacon and place in a microwave-safe pie plate. Drizzle bacon with honey; cover with plastic wrap. Just before serving, cook in the microwave for 30 seconds.

Heat olive oil in a large pot and gently sauté the onion, celery and garlic until fragrant. Stir in vegetable broth, parsnips and salt, and bring to the boil.

Reduce heat and simmer for 30 minutes. Set aside to cool and blend until smooth. Garnish with croûtons, fresh thyme and chopped bacon.

Fast Red Lentil Soup

Serves: 4-5

Prep time: 15 min

Ingredients:

1 cup red lentils

1/2 small onion, chopped

2 garlic cloves, chopped

1/2 red pepper, chopped

3 cups vegetable broth

1 cup coconut milk

3 tbsp extra virgin olive oil

1 tbsp paprika

1/2 tsp ginger

1 tsp cumin

salt and black pepper, to taste

Directions:

Gently heat olive oil in a large saucepan. Add onion, garlic, red pepper, paprika, ginger and cumin and sauté, stirring, until just fragrant. Add in red lentils and vegetable broth.

Bring to a boil, cover, and simmer for 15 minutes. Add in coconut milk and simmer for 5 more minutes. Remove from heat, season with salt and black pepper, and blend until smooth. Serve hot.

Mediterranean Lentil Soup

Serves: 4-5

Prep time: 20 min

Ingredients:

1 cup red lentils

2 carrots, chopped

1 onion, chopped

1 garlic clove, chopped

1 small red pepper, chopped

1 can tomatoes, chopped

½ can chickpeas, drained

½ can white beans, drained

1 small celery stalk, chopped

6 cups water

1 tbsp paprika

1 tsp ginger, grated

1 tsp cumin

3 tbsp extra virgin olive oil

Directions:

Heat olive oil in a deep soup pot and gently sauté onions, garlic, red pepper and ginger. Add in water, lentils, chickpeas, white beans, tomatoes, carrots, celery, and cumin.

Bring to a boil then lower heat and simmer for 20 minutes, or until the lentils are tender.

Puree half the soup in a food processor. Return the pureed soup to the pot, stir and serve.

Carrot and Chickpea Soup

Serves: 4-5

Prep time: 20 min

Ingredients:

4 carrots, chopped

1 onion, chopped

1 garlic clove, minced

1 can chickpeas, undrained

4 cups vegetable broth

3-4 tbsp extra virgin olive oil

1 tsp paprika

1 tsp grated ginger

salt and black pepper, to taste

Directions:

Heat olive oil in a deep soup pot over medium-high heat. Gently sauté onion, garlic and carrots for 3-4 minutes, stirring. Add in paprika, ginger, broth and chickpeas.

Bring to the boil then reduce heat and simmer, covered, for 10 minutes.

Blend soup until smooth and return to pan. Cook over medium-high heat until heated through. Season with salt and pepper to taste and serve.

Celery, Apple and Carrot Soup

Serves: 4-5

Prep time: 20 min

Ingredients:

2 celery stalks, chopped

1 large apple, chopped

1/2 onion, chopped

2 carrots, chopped

1 garlic clove, minced

4 cups vegetable broth

3-4 tbsp extra virgin olive oil

1 tsp paprika

1 tsp grated ginger

salt and black pepper, to taste

Directions:

Heat olive oil in a deep soup pot over medium-high heat. Gently sauté onion, garlic and carrots for 3-4 minutes, stirring. Add in paprika, ginger, celery, apple and broth.

Bring to the boil then reduce heat and simmer, covered, for 10 minutes. Blend soup until smooth and return to pan.

Cook over medium-high heat until heated through. Season with salt and pepper to taste and serve.

Pea, Dill and Rice Soup

Serves: 4

Prep time: 30 min

Ingredients:

1 (16 oz) bag frozen green peas

1 onion, chopped

3-4 garlic cloves, chopped

1/3 cup rice

3 tbsp fresh dill, chopped

3 tbsp extra virgin olive oil

fresh dill, finely chopped, to serve

salt and pepper, to taste

Directions:

Heat oil in a large saucepan over medium-high heat and sauté onion and garlic for 3-4 minutes.

Add in peas and vegetable broth and bring to the boil. Stir in rice, cover, reduce heat, and simmer for 15 minutes. Add dill, season with salt and pepper and serve sprinkled with fresh dill.

Minted Pea and Nettle Soup

Serves: 4

Prep time: 30 min

Ingredients:

1 onion, chopped

3-4 garlic cloves, chopped

4 cups vegetable broth

2 tbsp dried mint leaves

1 16 oz bag frozen green peas

about 20 nettle tops

3 tbsp extra virgin olive oil

fresh dill, finely chopped, to serve

Directions:

Heat oil in a large saucepan over medium-high heat and sauté onion and garlic for 3-4 minutes.

Add in dried mint, peas, washed nettles, and vegetable broth and bring to the boil. Cover, reduce heat, and simmer for 10 minutes.

Remove from heat and set aside to cool slightly, then blend in batches, until smooth. Return soup to saucepan over medium-low heat and cook until heated through.

Season with salt and pepper. Serve sprinkled with fresh dill.

Bean and Pasta Soup

Serves: 4-5

Prep time: 10-15 min

Ingredients:

1 onion, chopped

2 large carrots, chopped

2 garlic cloves, minced

1 cup cooked orzo

1 15 oz can white beans, rinsed and drained

1 15 oz can tomatoes, diced and undrained

1 cup baby spinach leaves

3 cups chicken broth

1 tbsp paprika

1 tbsp dried mint

3 tbsp extra virgin olive oil

salt and black pepper, to taste

Directions:

Heat the olive oil over medium heat and gently sauté the onion, garlic and carrots. Add in tomatoes, broth, salt and pepper, and bring to a boil.

Reduce heat and cook for 5-10 minutes, or until the carrots are tender. Stir in orzo, beans and spinach, and simmer until spinach is wilted.

Tuscan Bean Soup

Serves: 4-5

Prep time: 20 min

Ingredients:

1 onion, chopped

1 large carrot, chopped

2 garlic cloves, minced

1 15 oz can white beans, rinsed and drained

1 cup spinach leaves, trimmed and washed

3 cups chicken broth

1 tbsp paprika

1 tbsp dried mint

3 tbsp extra virgin olive oil

salt and black pepper, to taste

Directions:

Heat the olive oil over medium heat and gently sauté the onion, garlic and carrot. Add in beans, broth, salt and pepper and bring to a boil.

Reduce heat and cook for 10 minutes, or until the carrots are tender. Stir in spinach, and simmer for about 5 minutes, until spinach is wilted.

Lima Bean Soup

Serves: 5-6

Prep time: 3-4 hrs for soaking, 120 min for cooking

Ingredients:

1 lb dry Lima beans

4-5 cups water

2 leeks, white part only, chopped

1 small onion, finely cut

1 small celery stalk, chopped

3 carrots, chopped

5 cups vegetable broth

4 tbsp extra virgin olive oil

salt and black pepper, to taste

Directions:

Wash the Lima beans and soak them in water for a few hours. Discard the water, pour 3 cups of fresh water and cook the beans for an hour; discard this water too.

In a deep soup pot, heat olive oil and sauté the onion, leeks, celery and carrots until tender-crisp. Add 5 cups of vegetable broth and the Lima beans.

Stir, bring to the boil, lower heat and simmer for 1 hour. Season with salt and black pepper and puree half the soup in a food processor. Return the pureed soup to the pot, stir and serve.

Mediterranean Lentil and Chickpea Soup

Serves: 4-5

Prep time: 20 min

Ingredients:

1 cup red lentils

2 carrots, chopped

1 onion, chopped

1 garlic clove, chopped

1 small red pepper, chopped

1 can tomatoes, chopped

½ can chickpeas, drained

½ can white beans, drained

1 celery stalk, chopped

6 cups water

1 tbsp paprika

1 tsp ginger, grated

1 tsp ground cumin

3 tbsp extra virgin olive oil

Directions:

Heat olive oil in a deep soup pot and gently sauté onions, garlic, red pepper and ginger. Add in water, lentils, chickpeas, white beans, tomatoes, carrots, celery, and cumin.

Bring to a boil then lower heat and simmer for 20 minutes, or until the lentils are tender. Purée half the soup in a food processor. Return the puréed soup to the pot, stir and serve.

Curried Lentil and Parsnip Soup

Serves: 4-5

Prep time: 35 min

Ingredients:

1 cup red lentils

5 medium parsnips, peeled and cut into chunks

1 onion, chopped

1 garlic clove, chopped

2 large apples, peeled, cored and cut into chunks

6 cups vegetable broth

3 tbsp curry paste

3 tbsp extra virgin olive oil

Directions:

1 cup Greek yogurt, to serve

Heat olive oil in a deep soup pot and gently sauté onions, garlic and curry paste. Add the parsnips, lentils and apple pieces.

Pour over the vegetable broth and bring to a simmer. Cook for 30 minutes, or until the parsnips are soft and the lentils mushy.

Remove from the heat and purée the soup in a food processor. Return the to the pot, and serve with yogurt.

Italian Vegetable Soup

Serves: 4-5

Prep time: 25 min

Ingredients:

1/2 onion, chopped

2 garlic cloves, chopped

¼ cabbage, chopped

1 carrot, chopped

2 celery stalks, chopped

3 cups water

1 cup canned tomatoes, diced, undrained

1 1/2 cup green beans, trimmed and cut into 1/2-inch pieces

1/2 cup pasta, cooked

2-3 fresh basil leaves

2 tbsp extra virgin olive oil

black pepper and salt, to taste

Directions:

Heat the olive oil in a large pot over medium-high heat. Add the onion and cook until translucent, about 4 minutes. Add in the garlic, carrot and celery and cook for 5 minutes more.

Stir in the green beans, cabbage, tomatoes, basil, and water and bring to a boil. Reduce heat and simmer uncovered, for 15 minutes, or until vegetables are tender. Stir in pasta, season with pepper and salt to taste and serve.

French Vegetable Soup

Serves: 4-5

Prep time: 25 min

Ingredients:

2 leeks, white and pale green parts only, well rinsed and thinly sliced

1 large zucchini, peeled and diced

1 medium fennel bulb, trimmed, cored, and cut into large chunks

2 garlic cloves, chopped

3 cups vegetable broth

1 cup canned tomatoes, drained and chopped

1/2 cup vermicelli, broken into small pieces

3 tbsp extra virgin olive oil

black pepper, to taste

Directions:

Heat the olive oil in a large stockpot. Add the leeks and sauté over low heat for 5 minutes. Add in the zucchini, fennel and garlic and cook for about 5 minutes.

Stir in the vegetable broth and the tomatoes and bring to the boil. Reduce heat and simmer, uncovered, for 20 minutes, or until the vegetables are tender but still holding their shape. Stir in the vermicelli. Simmer for a further 5 minutes and serve.

Spiced Beet and Carrot Soup

Serves: 4-5

Prep time: 25 min

Ingredients:

3 beets, washed and peeled

2 carrots, peeled and chopped

1 small onion, chopped

1 garlic clove, chopped

3 cups vegetable broth

1 cup water

2 tbsp extra virgin olive oil

1 tsp grated ginger

1 tsp grated orange peel

Directions:

Heat the olive oil in a large stockpot. Add the onion and sauté over low heat for 3-4 minutes or until translucent. Add the garlic, beets, carrots, ginger and lemon rind.

Stir in water and vegetable broth and bring to the boil. Reduce heat to medium and simmer, partially covered, for 30 minutes, or until beets are tender.

Cool slightly and blend soup in batches until smooth. Season with salt and pepper and serve.

Creamy Cauliflower Soup

Serves: 4-5

Prep time: 35 min

Ingredients:

1 medium head cauliflower, chopped

1 garlic clove, minced

3 cups vegetable broth

1 cup milk

3-4 tbsp extra virgin olive oil

salt, to taste

black pepper, to taste

Directions:

Heat the olive oil in a deep pot over medium heat and gently sauté the cauliflower for 4-5 minutes. Stir in the garlic and vegetable broth and bring to a boil.

Reduce heat, cover, and simmer for 30 minutes. Add in coconut milk and blend in a blender until smooth. Season with salt and pepper to taste and serve.

Pumpkin and Bell Pepper Soup

Serves: 4-5

Prep time: 35 min

Ingredients:

1/2 small onion, chopped

3 cups pumpkin cubes

2 red bell peppers, chopped

1 carrot, chopped

3 cups vegetable broth

3 tbsp extra virgin olive oil

1/2 tsp cumin

salt and black pepper, to taste

Directions:

Heat the olive oil in a deep soup pot and sauté the onion for 4-5 minutes. Add in the pumpkin, carrot and bell peppers and cook, stirring, for 5 minutes.

Stir in broth and cumin and bring to the boil. Reduce heat to low, cover, and simmer, stirring occasionally, for 30 minutes, or until vegetables are soft. Season with salt and pepper, blend in batches and reheat to serve.

Mushroom Soup

Serves: 4-5

Prep time: 35 min

Ingredients:

2 lbs mushrooms, peeled and chopped

1 large onion, chopped

2 garlic cloves, minced

3 cups chicken broth

1 tsp dried thyme leaves

salt and pepper, to taste

3 tbsp extra virgin olive oil

Directions:

Sauté onions and garlic in a large soup pot until transparent. Add thyme and mushrooms.

Stir and cook for 10 minutes, then add the broth and simmer for another 10-20 minutes. Blend, season with salt and black pepper, and serve.

Spinach Soup

Serves: 4-5

Prep time: 35 min

Ingredients:

14 oz frozen spinach, slightly thawed

1 large onion, chopped

1 small carrot, chopped

1 small zucchini, peeled and chopped

3 cups hot water

4 tbsp extra virgin olive oil

1 tbsp paprika

salt and black pepper, to taste

salt, to taste

Directions:

Heat oil in a deep cooking pot. Add in the onion and carrot and cook for 3-4 minutes, until tender. Add in paprika, spinach, zucchini and water and stir.

Season with salt and black pepper and bring to the boil. Reduce heat and simmer for around 30 minutes.

Brown Lentil Soup

Serves: 4-5

Prep time: 35 min

Ingredients:

1 cup brown lentils

1 small onion, chopped

4 garlic cloves, minced

1 medium carrot, chopped

1 medium tomato, diced

3 cups warm water

4 tbsp extra virgin olive oil

1 tbsp paprika

1 tbsp summer savory

Directions:

Heat olive oil in a deep soup pot and cook the onions and carrots until tender. Add in paprika, garlic, lentils, savory and water, stir, and bring to the boil.

Reduce heat and cook, covered, for 30 minutes. Add tomato and salt and simmer for 10 minutes more.

Quinoa, Sweet Potato and Tomato Soup

Serves: 4

Prep time: 20 min

Ingredients:

½ cup quinoa

1 onion, chopped

1 large sweet potato, peeled and chopped

½ cup canned chickpeas, drained

1 cup baby spinach leaves

1 can tomatoes, drained and diced

3 cups vegetable broth

1 cup water

2 cloves garlic, chopped

1 tbsp grated fresh ginger

1 tsp cumin

1 tbsp paprika

2 tbsp extra virgin olive oil

Directions:

Wash quinoa very well, drain and set aside.

In a large soup pot, heat the olive oil over medium heat. Add the onions and garlic and sauté about 1-2 minutes, stirring. Add the sweet potato and sauté for another minute then add in the paprika, ginger and cumin.

Add water and broth, bring to a boil and stir in quinoa and

tomatoes. Reduce heat to low, cover, and simmer about 15 minutes, or until the sweet potatoes are tender.

Season with salt and black pepper to taste. Blend the soup and return to the pot. Add the chickpeas and heat through, then add the spinach and cook until it wilts.

Leek and Quinoa Soup

Serves: 4-5

Prep time: 15 min

Ingredients:

½ cup quinoa

3 leeks, white part only, sliced

3 garlic cloves, chopped

1 potato, cut in small cubes

½ cup canned chickpeas, drained

4 cups vegetable broth

1 cup coconut milk

2 tbsp extra virgin olive oil

½ tsp ground coriander

1 tsp turmeric

salt and black pepper, to taste

Directions:

In a large soup pot, heat the olive oil over medium heat. Add the garlic and sauté for 1-2 minutes, stirring. Add the spices and stir.

Add the broth and bring to the boil then add in the quinoa, leeks, chickpeas and potato. Reduce heat and simmer, covered, for 15 minutes. When the leeks are soft, add in a cup of coconut milk, stir, and simmer for 2 more minutes.

Red Lentil and Quinoa Soup

Serves: 4

Prep time: 20 min

Ingredients:

½ cup quinoa

1 cup red lentils

5 cups water

1 onion, chopped

2-3 garlic cloves, chopped

½ red bell pepper, finely cut

1 small tomato, chopped

3 tbsp extra virgin olive oil

1 tsp ginger

1 tsp cumin

1 tbsp paprika

salt and black pepper, to taste

Directions:

Wash and drain quinoa and red lentils and set aside.

In a large soup pot, heat the olive oil over medium heat. Add the onion, garlic and red pepper and sauté for 1-2 minutes, stirring. Add the paprika and spices and stir. Add in the red lentils and quinoa, stir and add the water.

Gently bring to the boil, then lower heat and simmer, covered for 15 minutes. Add the tomato and cook for five more minutes. Blend the soup, serve and enjoy!

Spinach and Quinoa Soup

Serves: 4-5

Prep time: 20 min

Ingredients:

½ cup quinoa

1 onion, chopped

1 garlic clove, chopped

1 small zucchini, peeled and diced

1 tomato, diced

2 cups fresh spinach, cut

4 cups water

3 tbsp extra virgin olive oil

1 tbsp paprika

salt and pepper, to taste

Directions:

Heat olive oil in a deep soup pot over medium-high heat. Add onion and garlic and sauté for 1 minute, stirring constantly. Add in paprika and zucchini, stir, and cook for 2-3 minutes more.

Add 4 cups of water and bring to a boil then add in spinach and quinoa. Stir and reduce heat. Simmer for 15 minutes then set aside to cool.

Vegetable Quinoa Soup

Serves: 4-5

Prep time: 20 min

Ingredients:

½ cup quinoa

1 cup sliced leeks

1 garlic clove, chopped

½ carrot, diced

1 tomato, diced

1 small zucchini, diced

½ cup frozen green beans

4 cups water

1 tsp paprika

4 tbsp extra virgin olive oil

5-6 tbsp lemon juice, to serve

Directions:

Wash quinoa in a fine sieve under running water until the water runs clear. Set aside to drain.

Heat olive oil in a soup pot and gently sauté the leeks, garlic and carrot for 1 minute, stirring. Add paprika, zucchini, tomatoes, green beans and water.

Bring to a boil, add quinoa and lower heat to medium-low. Simmer for 15 minutes, or until the vegetables are tender. Serve with lemon juice.

Tomato and Quinoa Soup

Serves: 4-5

Prep time: 35 min

Ingredients:

4 cups chopped fresh tomatoes

1 onion, chopped

1/3 cup quinoa

2 cups water

1 garlic clove, minced

3 tbsp extra virgin olive oil

1 tbsp paprika

1 tsp salt

½ tsp black pepper

1 tbsp sugar

fresh parsley, chopped, to serve

Directions:

Heat olive oil in a large soup pot and sauté onions until translucent. Add in paprika, garlic and tomatoes and water and bring to the boil.

Simmer for 10 minutes then blend the soup and return it to the pot. Add the very well washed quinoa and a tablespoon of sugar and bring to the boil again.

Simmer for 15 minutes stirring occasionally. Serve sprinkled with parsley.

Kale, Leek and Quinoa Soup

Serves: 4-5

Prep time: 35 min

Ingredients:

½ cup quinoa

2 leeks, white part only, chopped

1/2 onion, chopped

1 can tomatoes, diced and undrained

1 bunch kale (10 oz), stemmed and coarsely chopped

4 cups vegetable broth

3 tbsp extra virgin olive oil

salt and pepper, to taste

Directions:

Heat olive oil in a large pot over medium heat and gently sauté the onion for 3-4 minutes. Add in the leeks, season with salt and pepper and add the vegetable broth, tomatoes and quinoa.

Bring to a boil then reduce heat and simmer for 10 minutes. Stir in kale and cook for another 5 minutes.

Carrot, Sweet Potato and Chickpea Soup

Serves: 4-5

Prep time: 25 min

Ingredients:

4 large carrots, chopped

1 small onion, chopped

1 can (15 oz) chickpeas, undrained

2 medium sweet potatoes, peeled and diced

4 cups vegetable broth

1/2 cup milk

2 tbsp extra virgin olive oil

1 tsp cumin

1 tsp ginger

Directions:

Heat olive oil in a large saucepan over medium heat. Add onion and carrots and sauté until tender.

Add in broth, chickpeas, sweet potato and seasonings. Bring to a boil then reduce heat and simmer, covered, for 30 minutes. Blend soup until smooth, add milk and cook for 2-3 minutes until heated through.

FREE BONUS RECIPES: 20 Superfood Paleo and Vegan Smoothies for Vibrant Health and Easy Weight Loss

Kale and Kiwi Smoothie

Serves: 2

Prep time: 2-3 min

Ingredients:

2-3 ice cubes

1 cup orange juice

1 small pear, peeled and chopped

2 kiwi, peeled and chopped

2-3 kale leaves

2-3 dates, pitted

Directions:

Combine all ingredients in a high speed blender and blend until smooth.

Delicious Broccoli Smoothie

Serves: 2

Prep time: 2-3 min

Ingredients:

2-3 frozen broccoli florets

1 cup coconut milk

1 banana, peeled and chopped

1 cup pineapple, cut

1 peach, chopped

1 tsp cinnamon

Directions:

Combine all ingredients in a high speed blender and blend until smooth.

Papaya Smoothie

Serves: 2

Prep time: 2-3 min

Ingredients:

2-3 frozen broccoli florets

1 cup orange juice

1 small ripe avocado, peeled, cored and diced

1 cup papaya

1 cup fresh strawberries

Directions:

Combine all ingredients in a high speed blender and blend until smooth.

Beet and Papaya Smoothie

Serves: 2

Prep time: 2-3 min

Ingredients:

3-4 ice cubes

1 cup orange juice

1 banana, peeled and chopped

1 cup papaya

1 small beet, peeled and cut

Directions:

Combine all ingredients in a high speed blender and blend until smooth.

Lean Green Smoothie

Serves: 2

Prep time: 2-3 min

Ingredients:

1 frozen banana, chopped

1 cup orange juice

2-3 kale leaves, stems removed

1 small cucumber, peeled and chopped

1/2 cup fresh parsley leaves

½ tsp grated ginger

Directions:

Combine all ingredients in a high speed blender and blend until smooth.

Easy Antioxidant Smoothie

Serves: 2

Prep time: 2-3 min

Ingredients:

2-3 frozen broccoli florets

1 cup orange juice

2 plums, cut

1 cup raspberries

1 tsp ginger powder

Directions:

Combine all ingredients in a high speed blender and blend until smooth.

Healthy Purple Smoothie

Serves: 2

Prep time: 2-3 min

Ingredients:

2-3 frozen broccoli florets

1 cup water

1/2 avocado, peeled and chopped

3 plums, chopped

1 cup blueberries

Directions:

Combine all ingredients in a high speed blender and blend until smooth.

Mom's Favorite Kale Smoothie

Serves: 2

Prep time: 2-3 min

Ingredients:

2-3 ice cubes

1½ cup orange juice

1 green small apple, cut

½ cucumber, chopped

2-3 leaves kale

½ cup raspberries

Directions:

Combine all ingredients in a high speed blender and blend until smooth.

Creamy Green Smoothie

Serves: 2

Prep time: 2-3 min

Ingredients:

1 frozen banana

1 cup coconut milk

1 small pear, chopped

1 cup baby spinach

1 cup grapes

1 tbsp coconut butter

1 tsp vanilla extract

Directions:

Combine all ingredients in a high speed blender and blend until smooth.

Strawberry and Arugula Smoothie

Serves: 2

Prep time: 2-3 min

Ingredients:

2 cups frozen strawberries

1 cup unsweetened almond milk

10-12 arugula leaves

1/2 tsp ground cinnamon

Directions:

Combine ice, almond milk, strawberries, arugula and cinnamon in a high speed blender. Blend until smooth and serve.

Emma's Amazing Smoothie

Serves: 2

Prep time: 2-3 min

Ingredients:

1 frozen banana, chopped

1 cup orange juice

1 large nectarine, sliced

1/2 zucchini, peeled and chopped

2-3 dates, pitted

Directions:

Combine all ingredients in a high speed blender and blend until smooth.

Good-To-Go Morning Smoothie

Serves: 2

Prep time: 2-3 min

Ingredients:

1 cup frozen strawberries

1 cup apple juice

1 banana, chopped

1 cup raw asparagus, chopped

1 tbsp ground flaxseed

Directions:

Combine all ingredients in a high speed blender and blend until smooth.

Endless Energy Smoothie

Serves: 2

Prep time: 2-3 min

Ingredients:

1 frozen banana, chopped

1 1/2 cup green tea

1 cup chopped pineapple

2 raw asparagus spears, chopped

1 lime, juiced

1 tbsp chia seeds

Directions:

Combine all ingredients in a high speed blender and blend until smooth.

High-fiber Fruit Smoothie

Serves: 2

Prep time: 2-3 min

Ingredients:

1 frozen banana, chopped

1 cup orange juice

2 cups chopped papaya

1 cup shredded cabbage

1 tbsp chia seeds

Directions:

Combine all ingredients in a high speed blender and blend until smooth.

Nutritious Green Smoothie

Serves: 2

Prep time: 2-3 min

Ingredients:

2-3 frozen broccoli florets

1 cup apple juice

1 large pear, chopped

1 kiwi, peeled and chopped

1 cup spinach leaves

1-2 dates, pitted

Directions:

Combine all ingredients in a high speed blender and blend until smooth.

Apricot, Strawberry and Banana Smoothie

Serves: 2

Prep time: 2-3 min

Ingredients:

1 frozen banana

1 1/2 cup almond milk

5 dried apricots

1 cup fresh strawberries

Directions:

Combine all ingredients in a high speed blender and blend until smooth.

Spinach and Green Apple Smoothie

Serves: 2

Prep time: 2-3 min

Ingredients:

3-4 ice cubes

1 cup unsweetened almond milk

1 banana, peeled and chopped

2 green apples, peeled and chopped

1 cup raw spinach leaves

3-4 dates, pitted

1 tsp grated ginger

Directions:

Combine all ingredients in a high speed blender and blend until smooth.

Superfood Blueberry Smoothie

Serves: 2

Prep time: 2-3 min

Ingredients:

2-3 cubes frozen spinach

1 cup green tea

1 banana

2 cups blueberries

1 tbsp ground flaxseed

Directions:

Combine all ingredients in a high speed blender and blend until smooth.

Zucchini and Blueberry Smoothie

Serves: 2

Prep time: 2-3 min

Ingredients:

1 cup frozen blueberries

1 cup unsweetened almond milk

1 banana

1 zucchini, peeled and chopped

Directions:

Combine all ingredients in a high speed blender and blend until smooth.

Tropical Spinach Smoothie

Serves: 2

Prep time: 2-3 min

Ingredients:

1/2 cup crushed ice or 3-4 ice cubes

1 cup coconut milk

1 mango, peeled and diced

1 cup fresh spinach leaves

4-5 dates, pitted

1/2 tsp vanilla extract

Directions:

Combine all ingredients in a high speed blender and blend until smooth.

About the Author

Alissa Grey is a fitness and nutrition enthusiast who loves to teach people about losing weight and feeling better about themselves. She lives in a small French village in the foothills of a beautiful mountain range with her husband, three teenage kids, two free spirited dogs, and various other animals.

Alissa is incredibly lucky to be able to cook and eat natural foods, mostly grown nearby, something she's done since she was a teenager. She enjoys yoga, running, reading, hanging out with her family, and growing organic vegetables and herbs.

If you want to see other delicious and healthy family recipes that she has published you can check out her [Author Page](#) on Amazon.

Printed in Great Britain
by Amazon